REAL ESTATE INVESTING STRATEGIES

REAL ESTATE INVESTING STRATEGIES

By

JOE ARD

TABLE OF CONTENTS

ACKNOWLEDGMENT

This book would never have been written without the editing skills, support, encouragement, and patience of my loving wife Mary Ann.

Between 90 and 95 percent of real estate investors fail in the first year.

This is a large percentage; right now, you are probably wondering how this number can be so high. Someone must be getting lucky, sometime. Right?

Chance and luck are two partners you do not want to have to count on in real estate investing. They are nice to have, but they usually hang around the outskirts of planning, good judgment, best practices, and hard work. Unfortunately, they often take all the credit, which makes real estate investing look, to the outsider, fun, exciting—and easy. It can be a lot of things, but it's rarely easy.

This book is going to go over the most common traps of real estate investing to keep you out of the 90–95 percent club!

I have witnessed many traps over the past forty-one years while in the business of investing, and I can tell you it is difficult to avoid being eaten by the real estate wolves.

I am happy to share with you since I have been vulnerable to some of them. My investor friends have been vulnerable to certain scams. With permission, and without naming names, I will share their stories with you. None of us want you to fail or lose your money by acting unwisely.

This book is for the new real estate investor who is beginning or thinking about a journey in the world of investing. To succeed, it is vital you start in the right direction. Let me help you.

This book is not for the investor who already owns a portfolio of properties unless, like myself, you are often asked for advice. But this book is an excellent source for seasoned investors and

Realtors to share with clients who want to break into the real estate investing (REI) market.

Martin, a friend and real estate investor from Georgia, says, "Pay attention to Joe's words of wisdom and follow his real estate advice. This book will make you think before you act."

My guarantee: You will save thousands of dollars during your startup when you implement the principles and best practices illustrated in this book.

Do not be the next victim of the self-proclaimed "Experts" and their traveling show. Stop chasing real estate dreams, and make solid, planned real estate investments.

Finally, this book is not just talk. It is based on the most common failures and mistakes thousands of real estate investors make every day. Avoid the traps.

INTRODUCTION

"**A**re you a real estate expert?"

I get asked this question all the time and the answer is: I keep trying. I've made mistakes and I've made money. I would like you to make money and make fewer mistakes; my expertise is in what not to do when investing in real estate. When you follow the examples in this book, you will increase your odds of being on the plus side. That means cash flow—and that is the difference between success and failure in REI.

Most people have the misconception that REI is simple. Many define REI as follows: "Buy property using someone else's money. Put a tenant in the property. Pay for the property using the rent you collect every month and have a positive cash flow."

Trust me when I say it's not that easy. There are many variables in this scenario. You need to understand the various parts of the deal and the details of the fine print, then you will be prepared to make decisions, to move forward, and make a smart purchase for yourself and/or your family.

Thus, a better definition would be:

REI involves the purchase, ownership, rental, management, and/or sale of real estate for profit. Real estate is highly cash flow dependent.

The two main reasons for failure in real estate are negative cash flow and undercapitalization.

The most successful real estate investors know the basic pitfalls of investing and apply them to every transaction; no exceptions. Ever.

So instead of telling you how easy it is to be a real estate investor and what to do, I will focus on avoiding the pitfalls. This book explains in simple, logical terms the most common mistakes investors make—the mistakes that make it difficult to succeed in REI. Most investors (including me) learned the hard and most expensive way, but I want you to have the chance to learn from my mistakes and those of others. I want you to take a giant step toward success knowing the basics.

When the concept of this book was first on the horizon, I received a great deal of feedback about how and what I should include in a real estate book.

I was told that I was not "up" enough or "positive" enough to be a successful author. That no one wants to hear "what not to do." This advice may be true, but I also know business is not all positive. I have seen slumps, and you need to know how to stay in business when they hit. Business is not all "up" and business is not just about the good times. The same basic principles and best practices that get you to the top will also sustain you during the rough spots. This is the reason I want you to have a good foundation; it can make you or break you in difficult times. That's what you plan for. The easy times will take care of themselves.

This book may not express what you want to hear; in particular, it may not follow what others have told you in the past. I promise to share many years of experience with you about REI, and to explain the principles you need to know to be successful in your journey as a first-time investor.

This book will help you understand what not to do. If you apply the principles I describe and you are a serious, committed investor, you will increase your bottom line. I can't promise you anything other than this: these are tried and true standards of practice, that I and many others have found successful.

A group of fellow investors and I started a Real Estate Mastermind Group in 2000. At our meetings, investing issues often became a subject for discussion. We found the same topics came up on a regular basis. We also found principles and best practices often solved most of the difficult issues.

At one meeting, one of our partners said, "These actions should be called 'commandments,' not principles." Ever since, all of us in the group have called them commandments, because it reminds us of their importance in our decision making.

These commandments all address the triple constraints of our projects/investments and solve most of the problems and challenges we all have with our investments.

When I refer to addressing the triple constraints of an investment and/or project, I am talking about the supporting actions we implement in order to manage and control the constraints of:

- Time
- Cost
- Performance/Quality

These are your triple constraints. You must always know the driver of your investment/project. Which of the triple constraints will be the most important driver of the project? Which constraint will drive your actions and decisions? And no—they are not even. I don't care that you have at some point been led to believe they're all the same. They are not. You will have to choose; otherwise, you will never make a clear decision. Know the driver: time, cost, or performance/quality? They may be different for each REI and they may change within each investment. Just make sure you are the one making the changes.

In this book, the basic actions that address the triple constraints and make your investment successful are referred to as principles. These are the very basics that support your REI, and I believe they are the cornerstone of our industry. If you want to call them commandments, feel free to do so.

The purpose of this book is to share my experiences with first-time investors. This book was not written to tell you what to do or how to invest in real estate. It was written for two reasons: to help you understand what not to do and to ask you to consider certain principles, clear your head, and think before you act.

This book is based on the good and bad decisions I and others have made over our investment careers. It is a summary of the thousands of questions I have asked and been asked. More importantly, it is a summary of the top mistakes real estate investors still make.

Of all the questions, what most of us really want to know is: "What does it take to succeed as a real estate investor?"

This book is about success. It has advice, stories you can learn from, and a foundation built on best practices. Take the advice that suits you and learn from it. Use the basic principles and build your own investment platform. Observe the commandments, but choose your own path.

By the end of this book, you will have learned something about yourself. What you will be happy investing in; your next steps; and what things you plan on never doing. My hope is that you will also have an active list of things you plan on always doing, every single time you invest in a property.

I respect you the reader—and anyone else who wants to learn more about investment in real estate—to share not just the hype but the business sense. Because that is what REI is: a business. You need to treat it as a business from the first day.

Taking an idea from the Mastermind Group, at the end of each chapter I will ask you a "thinking question." Use this space as you wish. Take notes, answer the question and/or ask yourself more questions. I want this book to be a growth process for you and to motivate you to be a better investor. Push yourself to the next level.

I want you to write down your thoughts as you read this book. Do not write down or copy what is written, but instead write down what you are thinking at the moment about REI and/or you as an investor.

Let the journey begin.

MEN OF GENIUS ARE ADMIRED. MEN OF WEALTH ARE ENVIED. MEN OF POWER ARE FEARED, BUT ONLY MEN OF CHARACTER ARE TRUSTED.

ALFRED ALDER

CHAPTER 1

MYTHS, CHALLENGES, AND MISTAKES OF REI

In this chapter, I won't try to discuss all the myths, mistakes, and challenges involved with real estate; I will only hit on the top few—the deal breakers toward getting started. I will speak to the general rule—there will always be exceptions, but this book is not long enough for me to discuss them all.

MYTH: REI is easy!

At least this is what you see and hear at midnight on television. Someone shouts, "Buy with no money down and watch your bank balances grow!" Sounds great, doesn't it?

TRUTH: REI is not easy. With the proper guidance and planning, you can be successful. A key point I want to stress is this: to be successful you must treat investing as a full-time job. If you plan to succeed, REI is not something merely to dabble in. I refuse to fill you with hype. I want you to know what is in store for the long haul, and to look at the biggest challenges real estate investors face. I've been a licensed real estate agent for the past nineteen-plus years; sixteen of those years were as a real estate broker and founder of my own company. But it was never my intention to make REI a career. I'm going to tell you a short story about how I became interested in REI. You see, you and I are not so different. It all started with a book . . .

I grew up in Oxford, Mississippi, and in 1974 I graduated from the University of Mississippi. I spent the next couple of years in various, low-paying "corporate" jobs. I really did not feel I was getting ahead; my dream was to go to law school, but the problem was I had no money. I decided to join the US Army for the GI Bill benefit. On December 1, 1975, I enlisted.

My plan was to serve two years and then return to school, but the two-year plan turned into a twenty-two-year plan. While in basic, I was asked if I wanted to go to Officer Candidate School (OCS). They didn't need to ask me twice.

Off I went to OCS; after thirteen-weeks of school, I was a brand new commissioned Second Lieutenant (2LT).

My first assignment was in Korea, where I was stationed for eighteen months. Every month our unit received a magazine called *VFW Magazine* and every month I read that magazine from cover to cover; there was not much going on for me in Korea in 1977! I even read the advertisement on the back cover. It was for a book, *How to Wake Up the Financial Genius Inside of You*, written by Mark Haroldsen.

Eventually I needed something else to read, so after seeing this advertisement for months, I ordered the book. Was I ever happy to see that book in the mail!

It was a book on real estate, in which Mr. Haroldsen emphasized goal-setting as the most important aspect of investing. From the day I read the chapter on goal-setting, I have continued to always write down my goals. Big goals, little goals, long-term goals, short-term goals. All of them.

My first written goal back in Korea was: to buy a property within six months of my return stateside.

My next assignment, in June 1978, was to Fort Benning in Columbus, GA. True to my goal, I went to work with a Realtor who knew the area . . . and I bought my first property.

It was nothing fancy: two bedrooms, one bath. An all-brick house in a nice neighborhood. I bought it using my 100 percent, no-money-down VA loan. It cost me approximately $300 out of pocket and my payment turned out to be $81 a month.

So there you have it. How did I start my REI career? I read a book. Wrote down a goal. Followed up on my goal. I followed this process time and again as the Army assigned me to many locations for over twenty-two years. Long before I thought of taking the Realtor or broker exams, I become an investor. Thank you, Mr. Haroldsen.

Let's get back to the present.

Over the past nineteen years, I have given countless seminars. During these seminars, one of the first activities for our participants is to fill out a questionnaire. It asks the following, "What are your two biggest challenges as an investor?" We collect the responses at the first break and discuss the top issues at the end of the session.

Here are the top challenges in no particular order:

- Finding a good Realtor.

- Finding my first investment property or additional properties.
- Finding a good management company.
- Finding a good repair person.
- Finding a good tenant.
- Finding a good teacher/mentor.

I find it interesting that these six continue to surface, no matter where the market is—up or down. These six challenges always appear troublesome, and it's safe to say you, as an investor, will face some, if not all, of these challenges as well.

I've faced these challenges as a first-time investor and as a seasoned investor, and I know them to be recurrent—but we all get better at overcoming, preparing and facing challenges with time and experience. As you learn good investment basics/best practices, your ability to manage and avoid risk will improve. You need to avoid the risks associated with your investments as much as possible, and you need to manage the risks you cannot avoid. Most of all, you need to be able to identify the risks.

- Identify the risk. When done early, the result to your project budget is often low cost or no cost at all.
- Avoid the risk. You can decide to not proceed with the project or put into place alternatives to the risk. This decision often results in lower costs and at times no cost.
- Manage the risk. You can manage the risk by buying insurance, which can lower the cost of a risk and often costs less than the impending risk.
- Wait for the risk to happen or occur. Because you are working from an in-the-moment decision mode, which

is very stressful for you and the project. This type of action often results in high cost or even project failure.

Do REI principles change? I don't think so. The way they are presented or the media that is used changes continually, but the basics are always the basics, and you will always need them. There are no shortcuts. These remain the number one all-time principles: buying a property, making repairs, renting (having someone else pay the mortgage for your property), and management.

The keys to success are understanding the pitfalls of investing, establishing goals, and having a plan—a plan you can work from based on the principles explained in this book. A plan where you are in control. A plan where you manage your money. A plan that is clear. A plan that has few unknowns.

You must start with a plan.

Now that you are aware of the myths and challenges, let's consider the mistakes.

The most common mistakes new investors make, in my opinion, are:

- Paying too much for a property.
- Having negative cash flow and/or going into business undercapitalized.
- Being too trusting/paying a self-proclaimed expert for dead-end advice.
- Not working with a knowledgeable local Realtor to purchase a property.
- Buying their first property from a wholesaler.
- Not researching the true value of the property.

- Not obtaining an estimate for the cost of improvements and repairs.
- Learning to be a landlord by trial and error.
- Practicing inadequate property management.
- Starting too fast—no education.

As we proceed further into the principles of REI, we will face other challenges, and they apply to each investment to a lesser or greater degree. It is not a question of whether you will face challenges, but of how you will react to them.

When I started as an investor, the basic principles were explained/taught with a book and a good Realtor/mentor. Today we have an abundance of media: infomercials, internet, webinars, downloadable books, podcasts, blogs, and thousands of self-proclaimed REI gurus.

Do your research. Understand the basic challenges, mistakes, and myths that come along with each investment. And—you guessed it—have a plan. Knowing your weak points will help you move forward with success. Don't wait for it to happen. Understand your investment well enough to know what is coming next week, next month, next year. Be ready.

Thinking Question

After reading this chapter, what do you think will be your biggest challenge in REI?

WHEN THE STUDENT IS READY, THE TEACHER WILL APPEAR.

ZEN PROVERB

CHAPTER 2

HAVE A PLAN AND SET WRITTEN GOALS

This chapter explains how having written goals will increase your chances of success.

I talk to over a hundred people one-on-one every year about buying an investment property and becoming a first-time investor. The first question I like to ask is, "What is your goal?" And the most common response is, "Goal? I don't know."

Many have clear realistic goals, but many do not. I believe if a person does not have a written goal, achieving the desired results is going to be tough. So immediately, I give them a paper and pen and say, "Right now, before we go any further, write down at least three goals you want to achieve during your life." They think I'm crazy, but 99 percent of the time they write something down.

I get all sorts of answers:

- Quit my day job (probably #1).
- Become a millionaire in five years.
- Retire in ten years.

- Provide a service that makes a difference.
- Make a moderate to high income.
- Become a better husband and father.
- Play more golf.
- Make $500,000 this year.
- Travel internationally.

—and many other great ideas.

But, believe it or not, some people say they have no goals! I remind them subconsciously, we all have goals; some call them "a purpose" or "dreams." This is the failure point of a great many investors, the stopping point; they have a dream, but take no action. Without action, nothing can move forward. The dream is just the jumping-off point. Don't think you can just dream and go. It's more like: have a dream, make it a goal, do the research that will turn your goal into a plan, and then your plan will be an action toward success. Without action, your goals will never become a reality.

After they write down their real estate goals, my question to the would-be investors is, "What is your plan?"

If your answer is, "I don't have a plan," then you need to make one.

Imagine for a minute that you stop reading this, get in your car, and start driving. You drive within the speed limit and keep driving. Where are you going? What's the point?

I'm sure you would agree getting in your car and just driving is pointless. If you don't know where you're going, you'll probably find yourself someplace you don't want to be. It might be a pleasant place, or a tolerable place, or an awful place. But it will not be a place of your choosing.

This is how life can be without a plan. If you don't know where you want to go, your life can feel aimless, directionless, and meaningless. There's a huge difference between people who know where they want to go in life and those who wake up every day with no direction. People who know what they want out of life may not get everything, but those who have no idea what they want must take whatever chance gives them.

You already know how I feel about goals, so it should come as no surprise that I have made many plans over the years. One of my goals in the early years—besides buying my first investment property—was to be debt-free. This was not a goal I achieved quickly, and that is a point I would like to stress: everyone should have not only short-term but long-term goals. Never lose sight of the big picture.

Start with goals and develop a plan to achieve them. I want you to think differently, to change your mindset. Your goals are achievable. Prioritize each goal as you place them into your plan. Set an estimated date for each goal to be completed.

Now go to each goal in the plan and write down every action you can think of that is needed to achieve each one.

I am a college football nut. I look forward to my Saturdays. Let's put this goal/plan deal in perspective.

Clemson just won the 2018 College National Football Championship, beating Alabama. Both teams had the same goal of winning. If you're imagining both head coaches saying to their assistants when they got to the game, "Well, what's the plan?" then you're wrong; they had a definite game plan long before kickoff. Did they know the exact order of plays to be run? No. They adjusted their plan as required as the game went along. Both teams had practiced established principles. Both teams had a foundation to play from.

Dream, set goals, make a plan, execute the plan, and be prepared to make changes along the way.

Plan of Action: Write Out Three Real Estate Goals.

Need some help? Here's an example:

1. Acquire one investment property within the six months of my tour of duty in Korea.
2. Acquire ten investment properties in the next ten years.
3. Increase my net worth by $100,000 in the next ten years.

These were my written investment goals when I started back in 1978. They were pretty lofty goals for a twenty-four-year-old, but I was inspired at the time and never considered I would fail. I had a written goal. I was going to make a plan. I was on my way!

Be excited. I want the same for you. These goals are for you, right now. Be expressive. If there is something you have always wanted in life—now is your chance to write it down. Go for it.

These are your life goals. They may have nothing to do with real estate. You may want to take your family on vacation, or pay for your children's college education. For me, one of my life goals was to give back. That's what I'm trying to do with this book. If I can help someone become interested or motivated, or save them some heartache, I will have given back some amount of knowledge. I will feel in some small way that I have given back.

DO IT NOW!

In my life, I want to achieve these goals:

1.

2.

3.

Congratulations! Just the act of writing down your goals sets you apart from 97 percent of the rest of the world. In 1953, Yale University asked their graduating class what their goals were and discovered that only three percent of the students had any written goals. Twenty years later, Yale surveyed that same class and found that the three percent who had written their goals had earned more money than the other 97 percent combined.

Thinking Question

What are your REI goals?

UNTIL YOU BELIEVE IN YOURSELF, YOU WON'T BELIEVE IN YOUR FUTURE.

ANONYMOUS

CHAPTER 3

MY STORY: HOW I BECAME AN INVESTOR

Remember that nice little house from chapter 1? After I had been in the house for a couple of months, a friend of mine wanted to rent a bedroom. He said he would pay me $50 a month plus half the utilities.

- Let's do the math:
- Rent $50
- Military housing allowance $90
- Rent plus housing allowance = $140
- House payment $80
- Positive cash flow = $60

I was encouraged from my first buying experience. I later acquired two additional houses in Columbus by a process of assuming VA mortgages—about $400 out of pocket—with the help of a good agent, an excellent teacher/mentor who knew property management and owned a property management company. Realize this was in the past, and the money out of pocket may be different in the present day.

After expenses I was making around $300 per month cash flow. During the next twenty years, the Army moved me many times and I repeated the process several times before retiring in Atlanta, GA.

So that's how I got my start—the key point being that I had a good Realtor who guided me through the process of home buying.

Thinking Question

Ready to get started?

SOME PEOPLE DREAM OF SUCCESS, WHILE OTHERS GET UP EVERY MORNING AND MAKE IT HAPPEN.

WAYNE HUIZENGA

CHAPTER 4

THE #1 MISTAKE NEW INVESTORS MAKE, OR THE ONE PERCENT RULE.

In chapter 1, I stated that the number one mistake investors make is paying too much for an investment property. How do you know if you are paying too much? A good rule is to determine if the property meets the one percent rule.

The one percent rule is this: when you purchase a property, you will be able to rent it for 1 percent of the purchase price.

For example, if you purchased an investment/rental property for $150,000, the rent would be $1,500 per month. In my market (Atlanta), it is currently challenging to find properties meeting the criteria of the one percent rule. Real estate prices are at an all-time high. You make money when you buy the property (buy low), not when you sell it (sell high). In the words of Warren Buffett, "Be fearful when others are greedy and greedy when others are fearful."

I am fearful—or should I say, overly cautious—in the Atlanta market. Beware of someone telling you "this is a great deal" in any market. If it is such a great deal, why aren't they buying it?

Many people tell you anytime and any market is a good time to invest in real estate; I agree 100 percent, if you are buying your first home. You need to get prequalified, work with a Realtor, and get in the business of home ownership. In other words, stop making your landlord rich. You can probably own a home for about the same amount you are paying in rent.

The one percent rule is used when an investor is trying to decide if the market can hold up to the price of the property. Will you be able to charge enough rent in that area or property market to make your investment profitable? If you have to ask less than 1 percent rent, the property will not be profitable in the long run and most investors will tell you to walk.

Just because the market is bull in one area does not mean it is a bull market in *your* area. Even in the same state, the markets may differ. At the time of writing of this book, my area is a seller's market. Not so great for investors, and it's tough to make the one percent rule stick. Yet my partner is kicking butt in the southeast of the state, just 350 miles away. There's no problem meeting the rule there.

Thinking Question

Do you know the one percent rule? Do you understand why investors use it?

GIVE SOMEONE FIFTY SLIDES AND TAKE THEM FIFTY MILES FROM HOME, AND YOU HAVE AN EXPERT.

EDWIN MEESE

CHAPTER 5

THE MONEY TRAP

There is a saying we have all heard and use: "If it sounds too good to be true, it probably is." This saying is never truer than when applied to the self-proclaimed "real estate guru" or what I call, "real estate evangelists" (REE). What is a REE? These are the groups, firms, and companies who spout off about real estate and investing with such vigor and enthusiasm, it makes your head spin.

You hear their spiel, and it's natural to get excited because that is what real estate evangelists' seminars are about: getting the room jazzed up. They are about investing.

During the last ten–fifteen minutes is when they zig you. Now, it is all about the upsell and getting your money! You're told to sign up for a three-day course to get their "real" information. Only then will you learn how to make real money. Your free seminar just became a $1,500 investment. (Only $2,000 if you want to bring your spouse. What a deal!) But wait, don't you want to be a big-time investor while using someone else's money? Don't you want to make the "big" bucks? They have all the answers.

This three-day course quickly becomes a five-day course—for only $3,500! Of course, they offer a spouse discount. Even better, they provide tapes, videos, and blogs to read and watch at home.

That's a good thing because you'll be home a lot. Considering the generous discounts they offer, plus or minus the tapes and other media opportunities, you have now invested approximately $7,000:

Free talk:	$0,000
Three-day course (with spouse):	$2,000
Five-day course (with spouse):	$3,500
CDs, blog page, coaching sessions:	$1,500
TOTAL:	$7,000

Now, remember you've yet to invest a dime in real property. So how do you recoup your investment? You can't reach out to the gurus because the road show moved on to another town. They are still selling the hype. Again taking people's five–seven grand. They never invest in any real property; they just talk about investing. After all, the shows are more hype and talk than substance. Remember the presenters are not required to be licensed Realtors, brokers, and/or investors.

The people who fall for it are where they make their money. It is not in real estate. This is where I confess that I go to the free seminars. Now, wait. Before you get on your high horse, know that I'm only interested in knowing what they are saying and selling. I do not sign up for anything beyond the first free night. If you go to a seminar, please do the following to ensure you don't get caught up in the hype:

1. Ask for a copy of everything you sign. You will be asked to sign a registration card.
2. Pay close attention to the disclaimers.
3. Leave your wallet, checkbook, and all credit cards at home. Take only your driver's license.

I can't stress this enough. Don't think you won't fall for the hype and choose to bring your money. We can all be enticed by the professional evangelist. These are excellent performers. They do their jobs well. Otherwise, they would be out of business, and I would have nothing to write about.

I too have been lured in by the evangelists. When I started my investment career, I spent several thousand dollars on books and tapes, giving only a general knowledge of REI. I was armed with the theories but had no idea where to start finding investment opportunities. Soon, I became frustrated and wondered why I was failing. Essentially, I had the knowledge but did not know where to look for the deals. My problem was that I had given my money to the "real estate evangelists." The evangelists taught me the theories but could not show me the deals.

Let's look at an analogy I like to call the "Deer Hunting Theory."

A fast-talking "hunter" from Huntersville comes to Atlanta and gives a deer hunting seminar. He shows you many pictures of trophies he harvested and promises success if you follow his techniques.

At the end of the seminar, you're excited and armed with information about a web page and a blog. You bought everything they offered you. It seems to take a lot of stuff to be successful in this so-called easy process.

Next thing you know, you're standing in the parking lot, dressed from head to toe in baggy camouflage, with all your paraphernalia strewn about you: a big new bow, arrows, a long-range sight, photos of deer, graphs, a tape of deer sounds, and a deer caller. Do deer even make a sound?

You slowly look around the parking lot at all the people excitedly stuffing their vehicles with gear. The wild-eyed man parked next to you keeps repeating, "Where are the deer?" like a mantra. You find yourself shaking your head. "Beats me."

I believe all real estate is local. If you are going to put your money into your investment career, make sure you perform due diligence on the speaker and/or the company. Just as you will perform due diligence on the property you invest in, you should always consider where you place your money and time when it comes to your investment career. None of us have time or money to waste.

Chances are you will be buying in a local market. Are the speakers and/or experts local? Do they know the local and surrounding area? If not, are they willing to connect you with someone who does? Local experts' advice is always specific and informative, not general or vague.

Do not pay for a seminar unless the person is local. Remember to check them out online before paying. The out-of-towners are not familiar with your local market. I can assure you they do not know where the "deer" are.

There's another saying: "Give someone fifty slides and take them fifty miles from home, and you have an expert." This is the saying the evangelists live by.

I really could go on and on. I'm sure you can tell by now that this type of seminar is my biggest peeve when it comes to investors, especially new investors. Often, they're in this trap/scam before they realize it. Then it's too late.

I intended to print several scathing reviews here. Then I decided if you want to read bad reviews about real estate investment seminars, you can go online and find as many as you want. Read away. You will find useful and adverse reviews. Just be attentive; consider the fact most businesses don't print many bad reports, so when they do—pay attention. Enough said.

Yet there are the rare few who can enhance your real estate investment career more than you could ever imagine. When you make an investment in yourself and when you make an investment in real estate, due diligence pays off.

Before you give your money to any real estate expert or sign up for any seminar, check them out on the following websites:

Start by googling real estate scams

Second, I recommend www.ripoffreport.com

Third, I recommend www.real-estate-made-easy.com

I have gone into detail here about scams and real estate investment seminar evangelists. I have other words for businesses and people who take people's money in this manner, but evangelist is the word allowed in print.

I shared with you that I like to go on a free night and check the evangelists out. What is so heartbreaking for me is seeing the line of people signing up for the three-day course or the five-day course.

They are hoping to learn something that will give them a way in or a way out. Honestly, I wish I knew what they expected. The amount they pay for this upsell is good money they could be investing in real property. This could be an actual down payment. I only hope you're reading this book first, and not because you have already made the mistake.

When you go to your "free" seminar, take note of the assistants helping the main speaker. Usually, they are dressed in the same outfit; I call them the Green-Shirts. I want to ask them, "You look pretty sharp—why are you standing in the back? Why aren't you out making the million you are presenting week after week?"

Thinking Questions

What are some of the due diligence actions you already have in place to protect yourself and your investments?

At this point in the book, are there any actions you want to add or put into place to protect you and your investments?

THE MORE THAT YOU READ, THE MORE THINGS YOU WILL KNOW. THE MORE THAT YOU LEARN, THE MORE PLACES YOU'LL GO.

DR. SEUSS

CHAPTER 6

READ THE FINE PRINT

I want to look at learning the hard way.

Here is a situation I ran into full force. I was the man! I knew what to do! The mighty . . . how they fall.

I saw it in writing. There it was: "100 percent money back guarantee!" I read it again: 100 percent money back *and* you get to keep the books and tapes! How could this be a bad deal?

I plopped down the plastic so fast I almost sprained my wrist. I signed up for $599—but I could have 100 percent of my money back on request and I would get to keep the materials. Done.

I never saw it coming. And neither will you.

I arrived thirty minutes early, as instructed, and I waited in one of the four registration lines. As I stood there, I noticed maybe five to eight green-shirted individuals standing in the background. At the front of the line, I got verified and was given a stack of impressive books and a thick, blue bag to carry everything in, plus several tapes. I looked up just in time to catch the woman's broad smile as she said, "For safekeeping." She tucked my proof of purchase into my workbook cover.

Green-shirts sprang into action, directing us down the hall and into a long, narrow room, pointing us toward the rows of smartly lined, straight-backed conference chairs. Then, seeming overly happy with themselves, they disappeared.

With all the excitement of rushing here after work, everyone was blowing a lot of hot air. The room faced west and the curtains were wide open. Someone had forgotten to turn on the air conditioner. I glanced at my watch, bumped the lady next to me, and wondered what the odds were of me making it till ten o'clock.

Just as I was thinking, *This speaker better be damn good*, a tall, lean young man (yep, you guessed it: green shirt) strode to the middle of the room and tapped the mike. As if on cue, the loud rumble of a distant motor broke the silence, and the vents hissed a faint stream of cool air. The whole room sighed with audible joy.

We got through an hour of the slide presentation. The second hour, he droned on about nothing . . . I'm cutting to the chase . . . in the third hour, the smiley woman walked in and whispered in the speaker's ear. He says, "The seminar is over."

They both turned in unison and walked briskly—I mean briskly—off.

We all sat there. As the door closed, the air vents stopped blowing air, like they knew something we didn't. Now, I get it! I walked out to the lobby carrying my little blue bag of books and tapes. No one on site. Not a single green shirt in sight. Lock, stock, and . . . well, if there was a barrel, I am quite sure they took it.

But I have my receipt, right? 100 percent money back. Right?

Let me just mention here: I am not a man who is easily taken. I called, wrote, called again. I am Hot. Not like in the seminar hot; I mean, I am HOT.

What about your receipt, you ask?

Well, you see—that was where they had written, in tiny, tiny, *tiny* print: "You may request a 100 percent refund anytime before the seminar ends." Always read the fine print. You may need a magnifying glass!

I had that receipt for a long time. I thought about framing it, though I never did. No one likes to be scammed, but it keeps you humble, I guess.

Don't expect others to protect you. Read everything, even if it takes a long time; if people are waiting, let them wait. Take your time. If you don't understand something—anything—ask. Always ask!

My philosophy has always been: Don't Rush Me. Don't Push Me. I Don't Like To Be Pushed!

Thinking Question

Do you read the fine print?

YOU MUST GAIN CONTROL OVER YOUR MONEY OR THE LACK OF IT WILL FOREVER CONTROL YOU.

DAVE RAMSEY

CHAPTER 7

RESERVE FUND AND RETURN ON INVESTMENT

I want to explain the importance of having a reserve fund and how to estimate your Return on Investment (ROI). Buying a property without a reserve fund is going in undercapitalized. Undercapitalization will put you under faster, and do more damage, than any evangelist.

The lack of funds can often bankrupt you because of the high risk; it is a soft number (unknown cost).

I stated earlier that this is a common trap new investors face—mainly because you have been told REI is easy and you don't need any money.

Do not purchase a property without a reserve fund. You should have a six-month reserve for every property you are buying, and you should retain that reserve for as long as you own the property.

The reserve should be based on the gross rent of the property multiplied by six. It's there to cover unexpected repairs and vacancies; just because the property is vacant and not bringing in funds, the mortgage company won't stop expecting the monthly payment.

You will have recurring maintenance and repairs on the property (consider investing in a home warranty to cover major repairs on things like HVAC systems, water heater, and major appliances). Do not fantasize about having great tenants who pay on time every month. It may happen, but you can't bet your family's future on it. Rather than taking risks, you need to manage them. The six-month reserve fund will get you through difficult situations. Now you are prepared for any foreseen or unforeseen events, instead of waiting for a crisis to happen and dealing with it ad hoc.

All investors want to know how much the net profit will be at the end of the month. Your net profit will determine your Return on Investment (ROI). This is the formula I recommend you use to determine the estimated ROI when purchasing an investment property (the 60 percent rule):

In this example, we purchased a property for $150,000. The bank loaned us $135,000 at 5 percent for thirty years.

Monthly payment (principal and interest) = $724

Now apply the one percent rule. In this case the rent would be:

$1,500 per month × 12 = $18,000 (gross rent).
Gross monthly rent of $1,500 × 60 percent = $900.

This is the estimated net rent before the mortgage is paid.

Where did the 40 percent go?

- Taxes
- Insurance
- Maintenance/repairs
- Vacancy
- Management

After you pay the bank the monthly payment of $724, you are left with a profit of $176 per month. $176 × 12 = $2,112 per year net profit, divided by my investment of $15,000 = 14 percent ROI.

Most real estate courses forget to mention the 60 percent rule. Instead, they tell you your return will be as follows:

$1,500 rent minus $724 = $776 per month or $9,312 per year, divided by $15,000 down payment, or 62 percent ROI before taxes.

Ready to sign up for the three-day course? Step right up!

You will be able to estimate what your ROI might be. This is a "soft" number, but it gives you an idea of what your investment return will look like. It will take several years to determine the actual ROI.

Understand that, when someone is predicting your future costs or future gains for you, it's an estimate using data. The estimate is only as good as the data used to achieve it. Know where the data is coming from and also realize the resulting number is subject to change.

Thinking Question

Do I have a reserve fund for my first purchase?

PERFECTION IS NOT ATTAINABLE, BUT IF WE CHASE
PERFECTION, WE CAN CATCH EXCELLENCE.

VINCE LOMBARDI

CHAPTER 8

TENANTS AND TOILETS

Part One: You Buy the Tenant When You Buy the Property

Start thinking ahead. I want you to visualize the type of properties you want to own; get a picture in your head to go along with your goal. Set your standards. You don't want to buy just any property that comes your way.

Most new investors do not understand this concept. The "deal" is uppermost on the priority list. Often, new investors don't even think about what kind of property they should be looking at, or the area that will bring the best ROI.

Buy a profitable house in a nice neighborhood. The chance that you will find a good tenant who will take care of your property is much higher. You can make the one percent rule work if the property is in a good area with good schools. Remember we discussed the triple constraints: time, cost, and quality? These considerations all come into play with a less expensive property in an area without the right schools where you can't meet the one percent rule.

Buy a run-down property that cannot hold the one percent rule, and the odds are higher you will find a tenant who is Trouble with a capital T. At seminars, we tell everybody to look around the room. We ask the audience members to raise their hands if the people they see in the room are the kind of people they would like to have as tenants. All hands go up! Our response is, "Great! Start buying $200,000 to $500,000 properties!"

Our management company gets a call every week from an investor wanting us to manage their property. Most of the time, we refuse to take it on because the property is in lousy repair. Basically, this investor was sold a bad deal, and now he is stuck trying to be a landlord. It's always the same story. "Well, I was told when I bought the property that I could rent it for this much . . ."

Most of the time, you will be renting to families. Think about the schools in the area. Your tenants will be interested in them. Is it a busy street? Is there a lot of yard to maintain? Consider the type of tenant you want renting your property. What is your target market? That may help you decide where to buy.

As an investor, I will not buy a property that I would not live in myself. When I look for properties, I first consider the neighborhood, followed by the age of the house—the newer the better—then its condition.

Remember, in the introduction, I told you I was not a home inspector, but let's go look at a couple of potential rental houses. Visualize this in your mind. Get the picture.

We meet at my office. I am equipped with my flashlight and several sandwich bags. Before we even pull in the driveway of house one, we drive around the neighborhood. It's not looking good so far. I point out a vacant house with a couple of windows broken out; most yards are unkempt; some of the homes have metal bars on the windows; there are cars parked in the street and one house has been boarded up.

We pull in the driveway of house one. We might as well look at it now we're here.

First, we walk around the outside of the house, getting a visual of the following:

1. Condition of the roof from ground view.
2. Exterior paint and soffit wear (if I discover peeling paint, I will get a sample to test for lead-based paint; that's what the sandwich bag is for).
3. Type of siding.
4. Wood rot around the doors.

From our external visual inspection, it's not bad.

Next comes the interior walkthrough. We open the door and are greeted by the smell of smoke and pet urine . . . but being the adventurous house hunters we are, we venture further inside. There's no carpet in the house, but it still has a strong odor of mildew. I point out a water stain on the ceiling and I feel a dampness in the air. We keep hearing the roar of airliners passing overhead.

Because I want you to understand what to look for in the house, we enter the kitchen. The top of the stove looks like it has never been cleaned. I don't dare open the refrigerator. I open the cabinet doors under the sink . . . is that mold?

It's time to leave. No matter how you fix the house up, it will always be the wrong house in the wrong neighborhood.

This neighborhood is in a downturn, not an upswing; not a good market for a new investor. This is a high-risk property. I would not advise this kind of property for a new investor or first-time buyer, even if it looks like a good deal cost-wise. Sometimes there is something more important than a good deal: a successful deal. Start looking at long-term scenarios for each investment. If for some reason you needed to sell this property quickly, you could have a problem.

Let's go to house two—it's in a nice neighborhood, the yards are groomed. So far, so good.

We go in. There's no smell, no musky feeling in the air. The paint looks OK; the kitchen is clean; the bathrooms appear in good condition; there are no water stains; the carpet is a little worn and might need replacing. I think you should make an offer with a ten-day due diligence period.

Congratulations! You found your investment property!

Part Two: Beware of the Professional Tenant

In part one, we went through the house inside and out looking for obvious issues and deal breakers. In the next part, we're going to turn to the people who live there.

Why do tenants move? There are two primary reasons:

1. The neighborhood/schools.
2. The lack of response/maintenance by the landlord.

If you buy a house in a good neighborhood with good schools, your chances are greater of placing and retaining a long-term tenant.

I cannot stress this point enough. Tenants will pay a higher price to live in the right house in a good neighborhood.

I want you to get an understanding of the different types of tenants. No two tenants are alike, but most fit in one of three categories.

Category 1: Good Tenants—80 percent of all tenants. Good tenants pay on time—or, if they are going to be late, they call you, make arrangements with you and pay the late fee. They take excellent care of the property inside and out. They take care of small problems with the property, and they do not call in the middle of the night for petty maintenance requests. Good tenants are long-term tenants who treat the property as if it were their own.

They want to make it work as much as you do. Usually, they have children and would prefer to keep them in the right school system. They want to work with you, so work with them. Treat them well, and you will have an excellent long-term relationship.

There's a sub-category of these good tenants—Section 8 tenants—who are my favorite tenants of all. A Section 8 tenant is on a government program that subsidizes their monthly rent in whole or in part.

This is the way it works. First, it is guaranteed rent, paid by direct deposit. The tenant will find you; generally, they just call and ask if you take Section 8 Vouchers. You should ask the following questions:

- How much is your voucher for ($)?
- How many bedrooms are you authorized (family size determines the number of bedrooms)?
- When would you like to see the property?

If you like the tenant and the tenant wants the property, they will provide you with the paperwork required by the Section 8 Program. You fill it out, the tenant turns the paperwork in, an inspection is set up by the Section 8 Program, and after the house passes inspection, a move-in date can be set. If the house fails inspection, a list of required repairs is provided and a reinspection is scheduled.

A section 8 tenant generally requests less maintenance and fewer repairs, and takes outstanding care of the property. You may be wondering why. Well, if a person is on the program and gets kicked off or removed for any reason— including the destruction of your property—they are off the program *forever*! The fact that the Section 8 Program inspects the property several times a year ensures the tenant and landlord are maintaining the property. Win–Win. This tenant is generally a long-term tenant because once they find a property in a location they like, they are reluctant to move. For them, this is not just a rental, this is a home, and it works well for all concerned.

You bought well, and you found a great tenant. Now, repeat that action.

Category 2: Bad Tenants—15 percent of all tenants. The Bad Tenant is just the opposite of the Good Tenant. Consistently late with payments, they will destroy the property inside and out. They call to report every little maintenance problem, and when the repair crew arrives at the scheduled time, no one is home. Bad tenants generally move every year after trashing the property. This tenant will cost you money and create stress; all you can do is be glad they will be gone in a year.

Ideally, you don't want them at all, and so you must check and screen your tenants. I don't care how nice they look or sound. I don't care what kind of story they have—they will have one!

Category 3: Professional Tenants—5 percent of all tenants. The professional tenant is the one you never want to see, ever. A Professional Tenant is a real thing. They are out there—take my word for it. There is no need for you to experience this area of investment management firsthand.

This person knows the law and uses it to their advantage at every opportunity. This person knows the eviction process to the letter of the law. The professional tenant generally pays the first month's rent and one half month's deposit . . . and never pays again. Well—they will pay when they get the eviction notice, but it will only be a partial payment. And if the landlord accepts the partial payment during the eviction process, in some cases the tenant can stop the eviction process.

This tenant will also call in many bogus maintenance problems that do not exist, just to frustrate you. They will use the lack of response on maintenance calls as an excuse for not paying rent.

Remember, they know the law in your state/area—you need to know it too. These people are pros. They play for keeps. When you go before the judge, you better have your facts and procedures in order, or you stand an excellent chance of losing your case.

Again, I stress the importance of screening tenants to avoid being stuck with a professional tenant.

Just to give you an idea of why choosing the right tenant is so important: our management company spends 80 percent of the time dealing with 20 percent of our tenants, and it usually involves rent collection. It is our responsibility to work with the tenant and collect your rent.

I genuinely believe that every tenant but the professional tenant would pay on time every month if they could. We would prefer to work with the tenant and keep them in the property than to evict them, although we will do an eviction if necessary. On occasion, a property owner will scream and kick the tenant out, but what that owner fails to consider is that when a tenant moves out, the property has to be cleaned and maybe even painted. It could sit vacant for several months. Will you be better off if you give the tenant a chance to catch up, or if your property sits vacant? And what type of tenant is going to move in next? Most of the time, you are better off with a tenant willing to work with you.

Proper screening of potential tenants will eliminate most of the bad and professional ones, but on occasion one will slip through. Asking for references from the previous landlord is extremely important, but be aware that some landlords will tell you how great the tenant is just to pass his problem on to you—not often, but it happens.

Don't allow yourself to become desperate for a tenant—any tenant. A bad decision can cost you months of rent and repair costs. Take the time up front to make a good selection. You will be happy, and your tenant will be happy.

I hope this helped you understand the three types of tenants.

Part Three: The Challenge of Being a Landlord

Next, I want you to look at some of the pros and cons of being a landlord.

I tried being a landlord myself for a couple of years and I hated it. You, on the other hand, might enjoy getting calls in the middle of the night, on weekends, and while vacationing with your family. You will need to be available 24/7 for each of your rental properties, plus you will need to be a handyman, or have a handyman relative who will work on the cheap.

Let's take a look at tenant Mr. Smith, who lives at 100 Main Street, Summerville, GA.

He rings you Sunday evening at eight thirty because his air conditioner is not working.

You say, "I'll call someone Monday morning and let you know when he can come over."

Smith is not happy. "I can't sleep in this heat! Do you know the temperature in here? I have to work tomorrow. My kids need to sleep. They can't miss school."

What are you going to do? Do you have a repairman you can call? Well, now is the time to hit the Yellow Pages and start calling every air conditioning repairman in town. If it's

June, July, August, or September, you may get a service call out in a week.

You call the tenant, then go to a discount store, buy ten box fans, and deliver them yourself. Finally, when the repairman graces you with a visit, the unit is bad. The replacement costs and installation come to $3,000. There goes two months' rent, and the tenant wants a discount for the month.

Other maintenance calls you can count on include, but are certainly not limited to, the following:

- Stopped-up toilet
- Blocked kitchen sink and disposal issues

Better make friends with a plumber who responds to emergencies.

- A wild animal on the back porch or in the attic
- Bees in the attic
- Bats in the attic

You need a Critter Control guy, too.

- Light fixture does not work

You will be changing a lot of bulbs, unless you have a tame electrician.

Some tenants will rarely call; you may have to call them from time to time to make sure all is well, and ride by your property to inspect the outside condition.

But some are squeaky wheels. Often these are not "bad" tenants—they just need their hands held. This is your property, and often it's a good idea to regard their calls as an opportunity to check on your investment. Look around; is everything being taken care of? Make sure you don't need to take any action or fix something small before it gets out of hand. This is a chance to save yourself a call, or even some money down the road. If your property looks good—tell them, thank them. People like to be appreciated.

Another problem is the rent collection. The number one mistake is telling the tenant you own the property. As soon as they find out you are the landlord, emotions come into play, and all of a sudden, they stop paying rent. Tell the tenant you are just the property manager, or you may have this scenario:

You: "I was calling to ask why the rent had not been paid."

Tenant: "Really sorry, got behind, been slow at work. The company cut my hours. You will have it in a couple of weeks plus the late fee."

You: "OK, you've been a good tenant so far—I will work with you."

Two more weeks go by, and there's still no rent. You remember a real estate course you took a couple of years ago. Finally, you figure out what you think is the law regarding the eviction process, so you post a letter on the door and send another by certified mail demanding payment. Another week passes, you go to the courthouse and fill out paperwork to have the tenant served eviction notice by the Sheriff's Department. Another week passes, and you get a letter giving you a court date. The date is on your anniversary, and you have already booked a cruise. In the meantime, you get a check for half a month's rent, which you run to the bank and deposit. You cancel the eviction, you go on the cruise.

When you return, there's still no money, so you start the process over. It goes on and on. Are you getting the picture?

As for myself, I do not have the available time, nor do I have the skills, to tackle all the necessary repairs, so the management route was the perfect match for me—and it gave me more time to spend finding new investments. This is a better use of my time.

You may not need to jump into working with a management company right away with your first property, or even your second. If you have the extra time to spend on the management and feel you have the skills to handle most repairs yourself—go for it.

My advice—which has always worked for me—is to find a good management company that has a maintenance plan in place for routine and emergency repairs. Let them explain the eviction process to you and what it will cost if they carry out an eviction on your behalf.

I forgot to mention background checks, credit checks, setting up an escrow account for the deposits, and twenty other items.

There is one certainty in the rental business: if you have an empty property, you will get a lot of calls during the last week of the month. The caller will tell you they have to move by the end of the month; be sure to ask them why. Some of the time, it is because they are getting evicted.

If you decide to manage your own properties, then you must treat your tenants with the highest respect and take care of their homes. Again, I stress the following: never tell them you are the owner of the property—you are just managing it, and you don't get paid if the owner doesn't get paid.

If you do manage your own properties and start feeling overwhelmed and stressed, if the management side of your business starts taking over the REI side, you are probably ready to find a good management company. You are an investor, not a property manager.

Part 4: Property Management Can Make or Break You

This is an important decision you will make when you buy a property—more important than the property itself. It does not matter how excellent the investment is, or the location, or the rent. If it is not managed correctly, you won't get the ROI you were hoping for.

There are three questions you should always ask when you are hiring a management company:

- Do you screen your tenants?
- Do you perform a background check?
- Do you call the previous landlord?

The answer to all three better be yes! Additional questions you need to ask are:

- How many properties do you manage?
- How much would you rent my property for?
- How do I get my monthly rent?
- When do I get it?
- How much rental fee do you charge?

- How are maintenance and emergency repairs handled?
- Are your repair contractors insured, licensed, and bonded?
- Do you require the tenant to have renter's insurance?
- If you do an eviction, what is the total cost and who pays?
- Who turns on utilities in between tenants?
- Do you make any money off repairs?

Again, remember all real estate is local. My company generally manages only the properties that we sell to our investors. If you buy the wrong property in a bad area, don't ask us to manage it.

You can always find a company to manage your property. There are plenty out there who will charge you a flat monthly fee, whether the property is rented or not.

My advice is to find a management company that has a maintenance plan in place for routine and emergency repairs. Make sure they are clear on the eviction process and what it will cost you if they have to do an eviction on your behalf.

The best place to look for a management company is on Zillow.com.

Even if you have a great property, its management can make or break you. You have made positive decisions so far by due diligence and research. This is no time to slack off. Choose wisely.

Thinking Question

Are you prepared for tenants, landlording, and property management?

GOD PROVIDES THE WIND, BUT MAN MUST RAISE THE SAILS.

ST. AUGUSTINE

CHAPTER 9

TAKE ACTION

Now we come to the reason you purchased this book. Now you have goals, a plan, or at least an idea for a dream. You have a good idea of REI—what it is and what it is not. It's time to start the wheels moving. This is your start point.

This chapter explains the most challenging task in beginning your investing career. As with most ventures, starting is the most challenging task. If you want to be a real estate investor, you must purchase a property.

Many of you are already investors but do not realize it. If you own your primary residence—you are already an investor.

Home ownership involves:

- Qualifying for funding.
- Finding a property.
- Putting a property under contract.
- Closing the property.
- Routine maintenance.

- Property taxes and insurance.

As a property owner, you have the following benefits:

- Appreciation—hopefully your property will increase in value every year.
- Paying yourself—paying down your mortgage amount every month.
- Increasing your net worth—owning your home.
- Tax deductions—you can write off the interest you pay, so in many/most cases you will reduce the amount of taxes you pay.

If you already own your primary residence and are ready to begin acquiring property, try and find a Realtor who is also an investor.

Buying a rental is basically no different than buying your primary residence. It involves the same steps. The most significant difference is that you will be collecting rent and applying it to the mortgage on the property.

Step 1: attend a meeting put on by a local Real Estate Investment Association (REIA). Start at www.nationalreia.com; click on membership and find a local group.

Attend a monthly general membership meeting to get an overall feel for it. You will find everyone you need to get started: Realtors, lenders, hard money lenders, contractors, title companies, inspectors, wholesalers, pest control companies, and a dozen more vendors.

Go, observe . . . and do not buy anything. While they will offer plenty of free courses, in many instances, they will try to upsell you later. Spend the next couple of weeks researching the

REIA and attending a couple of sub-group meetings. You will begin to see the many aspects of REI.

I highly recommend joining an REIA—it's an excellent place to start building your real estate team. The members of REIA are there to help you; REIA is a team sport, and if you succeed, they will succeed.

Step 2: Before you even contact a Realtor or an individual about investing in a property, you must have your funding in place. In other words, you need money—either cash or some form of financing.

Get your financing in order and be sure you can qualify for a loan. This is a natural step for investors. The first step is to go to your bank and talk to a loan officer. That is their role—to loan money to qualified customers. Or if you don't like the bank idea, go and apply online.

OK, so you are qualified. What next?

Step 3: Find a Realtor. Where? According to the National Association of Realtors, there are over 1.2 million Realtors in the US. There is a real estate office on every corner. You see their advertising on billboards and on grocery store shopping carts. Believe me, they are everywhere, and you will have no problem finding one. You will meet plenty at the REIA.

Many of the 1.2 million I mentioned are part-time, which is not to say they are not qualified, but I recommend you find an excellent full-time Realtor who works with investors. Not your neighbor, not your Aunt Sue, not your Cousin Pete (unless they really are local investors).

Remember I dedicated a whole chapter to the Real Estate Evangelist? When you go to the free seminar, and they ask you to sign a registration card, get a copy of what you sign. You may be surprised. At an event I attended recently, this was on the disclosure in tiny, tiny print: "it is highly recommended that individuals work with licensed real estate brokers and/or agents for any specific, individual real estate transactions."

Even the evangelists say you should work with a Realtor!

Realtors sell property to make a living. They basically work for free until you close on a property, then they get paid a commission.

What do they do to earn it?

- Research properties for sale in your area.
- Prepare a comparative market analysis that shows you the current market.
- Spend countless hours driving you around, showing you properties.
- Provide information on the local area: schools, churches.
- Write and negotiate contracts for you.
- Set up inspections and appraisals.
- Arrange for a termite inspection.
- Set up the closing and close the property.

Realtors are required to be licensed by the state in which they sell a property. They must:

- Have a state exam.
- Be subject to state laws.
- Undertake continuing education.

Step 4: find a property. Explain to your expert Realtor the type of investment you want to make. They will show you properties in which you can invest, and you will determine if they meet the one percent rule. Continue to do your research before you decide to invest.

Many brokerages have property management companies. They will assist you in finding property management. When you get ready to buy, a Realtor will be glad to help.

Joe's general rules of investing:

1. Do not buy a property that you have not seen and physically walked through.
2. Only buy local real estate through a local Realtor.
3. For your first investment property, do not buy a property that you cannot drive to in less than forty-five minutes.
4. With more experience, you may buy outside of the forty-five-minute zone.

Most Realtors prefer to stay and play in their own playground. I sell real estate inside the greater Atlanta area. I don't sell real estate in Denver, Phoenix, Detroit, Dallas, or any other major market—but I can refer you to excellent Realtors anywhere in the US, and that's what any reputable Realtor should do for you.

Good agents live by the "Golden Rule" and know that if they help you, you will be a repeat customer and refer others to them. Some call it "Doing good business." Some call it "Would you do business with me again?" Whatever you call it, it means that if you are going to be successful in this business, you better follow this Golden Rule.

Learn the basic principles from me, and then buy from the Realtor who you determine, after your investigation, is the local market expert.

While 90 percent of real estate gurus sell books and seminars, a good Realtor will teach as well as providing timely, critical data to assist the investor in making excellent investment decisions. The decisions are in the data, not the feel-good promises.

Thinking Question

Do you have an expert local REI Realtor? Are you ready to get started?

ASKING QUESTIONS IS THE FIRST WAY TO BEGIN CHANGE.

KUBRA SAIT

CHAPTER 10

ASK A LOT OF QUESTIONS

In this chapter, I want to go over a list of questions you should ask when purchasing any property.

When you call your Realtor and tell them that you are an investor looking for an investment property, they will ask: what kind of property? What's your price range? Have you been prequalified or are you paying cash? Are you working with another Realtor? A Realtor will be able to determine if you are wasting their time. If you don't know the price range or type of property, if you have not been prequalified, or you don't have cash, you are wasting your time and theirs.

- The big question—are you working with another Realtor? If the answer is yes, the conversation may end. Most states require that you enter into a signed exclusive buyer/broker agreement. In GA, state law prohibits the broker from representing the buyer as a client without first entering into a written agreement with them. A summary of this six-page document could be as follows: When you sign this document, you agree to hire a Broker to act as Buyer's exclusive real estate broker in locating a property.

- There will be a time limit or term of this agreement.
- There will be a stated commission to be paid when you purchase a property.
- If you purchase a property from anyone (wholesaler, for sale by owner, your relative, at auction) during the term of this contract, you owe this broker their commission.

This is not a trap, but if you sign a ninety-day agreement, you are locked in unless the contract is terminated in writing by both parties. Most brokers will release you from this agreement, but some may not.

Set up a meeting with the Realtor to discuss your plan before you sign anything.

I like to meet my potential clients face-to-face in my office. We will set up a time to visit some properties and see if you feel comfortable working with me. I will also ask you to sign a one-day agreement allowing me to represent you.

Back to the deer hunting theory: don't go house hunting unless you are prepared to pull the trigger. The Realtor will be your guide. There will be other buyers competing for the same properties; if you see one that you like, move on it. Excellent properties in good neighborhoods do not stay on the market very long.

Remember to shop for a Realtor before you shop for a house. An excellent Realtor will save you thousands of dollars.

Here are the questions you may want to ask a Realtor before you decide to work with them. These are tough, so don't be surprised if they don't know all the answers:

1. Are you an investor, and how many properties do you own? If their answer is, "I am not an investor," you might consider looking for another Realtor. I don't care how nice this one is, or that you know his mother. You do not want to pay for his REI education.
2. Can you provide me a list of bank-owned and foreclosed properties in the local area? (This may be a tough question depending on what information is provided in the local Multiple Listing Service.)
3. How many bank-owned and foreclosed properties did your brokerage sell last year? They may not be able to answer how many the brokerage sold but then ask how many they personally sold in the past year. Don't be surprised if their answer is zero; it's not an indicator they cannot help you in your search.
4. The last question: Does your brokerage have a property management division? A small percentage of brokerages provide property management services, and the best case is to find a brokerage that manages what they sell.

After you find a property you are interested in, you will want to ask more questions:

1. What is the tax value? This is a public record. If they cannot give you this information, you really should find a new Realtor.
2. How many days has this property been on the market? This, too, is basic information.
3. What was the last sale date and price? Some agents cannot answer this question and say the data is unavailable. Find a new agent.

4. Can you give me a comparative market analysis or a list of comps in the area? This should be another simple task.
5. What will the property appraise for? This is a trick question. Unless the agent/Realtor just happens to be a licensed appraiser, the correct answer is, "I don't know, I am not an appraiser."
6. Who owns the property? At least 50 percent cannot answer this question, but any Realtor who deals with investment property should know the answer.
7. How was the listing price determined? If the property is a HUD, the answer should be, "by an appraisal." If the property is a bank-owned/REO, the answer is either, "by an appraisal" or, "by a broker's price opinion."

Once again: just ask some questions about every deal. Here are the questions to ask a wholesaler or individual selling a property:

1. Who owns the property? If the answer is "I do," check the tax records. If their name is not on the tax records—move on. If the answer is, "I have it under contract," then run, don't walk. Why? Because this person is looking for a quick flip. He has the property under contract only. He wants to sell to you at a higher price. He closes both on the same day and makes a fast buck. He is a paper pusher, not an investor. Just stay clear.
2. How did you come across this property? Ask if they are a Realtor. Just ask the same questions you would ask a Realtor.

If the house is listed in the local Multiple Listing Service, you can already know the answer to most of the questions above by going to Zillow.com and entering the property address. That's the best starting place to get information about a property.

One last thing: before you buy a property, you better have an exit plan. (What's an exit plan, you ask? Now you're learning!) An exit plan is having an idea of what you want to do with your new investment property. The two most common are rent and hold as an investment property, or fix up and flip.

Thinking Question

Are you prepared to ask a lot of questions?

BEFORE ANYTHING ELSE, PREPARATION IS THE KEY TO SUCCESS.

ALEXANDER GRAHAM BELL

CHAPTER 11

BANK-OWNED AND FORECLOSED PROPERTIES

When you are looking for a property, never tell a Realtor you are looking for a deal. Their response will probably be, "So am I—and if I find one, I'm going to buy it."

Some of the best pricing is found on foreclosed properties, and a great place to start looking for these properties is at www.hudhomestore.com, which also provides additional information on how to find and buy HUD homes.

What is a HUD property? A HUD property is a property that was funded using a federally insured FHA (Federal Housing Administration) loan. When a lending institution makes an FHA loan, and the property is foreclosed, the government makes good on the loan. Now the FHA, not the lending institution, is the owner of the property.

The property is turned over to HUD (Department of Housing and Urban Development) for disposal.

Some key points:

- All HUD properties for sale can be found at www.hudhomestore.com.
- HUD properties are sold through an online bidding process.
- You must use a Realtor who is registered with HUD.
- The Realtor will place the bid on your behalf.
- All properties are listed and sold through a HUD approved real estate broker.
- All HUD properties are sold as is, where is.

Let's look at what you get when you search for properties on HudHomeStore:

For my search criteria, I entered GA for the state and Clayton for the county.

My search showed a three bedroom, two bath house listed at $75,000 in Jonesboro, GA. I looked at the home on Zillow to get the value it put on the house. The Zillow estimate was $80,769.

My wife and I went to preview the house. We drove around the neighborhood and on a scale of A to D (A being the highest), we gave it a B+.

We were pleasantly surprised by the condition of the house. Our walk around the outside revealed the need for some minor wood replacement and repainting of the exterior. The air conditioning unit looked like the original and we thought it might need replacing. All of the shrubs around the house needed a proper trimming, to give the house better curb appeal.

The interior of the house was basically in move-in condition; there was no bad odor, the carpets were clean, appliances were present. It needed painting, but that was about all.

I took some pictures, and we decided that the house also was a B+ house, which meant we could live in it. (Remember I said I would never buy a property that I wouldn't live in?)

Here you have a $75,000 house! Not bad, no matter where you are, is it? There are buyable properties out there—you just need to search and do your homework.

Here are the actual pages copied from the HUD website, along with a copy of the MLS listing.

If you find a property you are interested in, begin by calling the listing agent on the house. When you get them on the phone, remember the previous chapter and ask a lot of questions.

The agent will also be asking you questions, such as:

- Are you working with a Realtor?
- Have you signed an agreement to work exclusively with a specific Realtor?
- Will you be paying cash or financing the property?
- When would you like to see the property?

After seeing the property, some new investors I have worked with have said things like, "Bid $40,000 and see if HUD will take it." But there will be many investors looking at this property and the high bid will win. So I politely reply, "HUD will not take $40,000 even if you are the highest bidder. I don't need practice submitting bids."

Owner occupants are given priority to bid and purchase the house. Your agent will tell you if the house is eligible for investor bids.

Note: If an agent places a bid on a property and you win the bid, you must submit proof of funds for a cash purchase, or a prequalification letter if you are financing the property.

I highly recommend working with a Realtor who can explain the HUD process. Chances are they are familiar with how to acquire bank-owned and foreclosed properties. If they cannot explain the process, find a new Realtor

Finally, a quick note on bank-owned properties. Go to Zillow and look up what the property foreclosed for. Sometimes the bank will accept a price less than the list price. It works like this: Joe financed $200,000 with the bank. The bank foreclosed on Joe's note for $190,000 and now it wants the property off its books. It has the house appraised and—due to a drop in the market or the condition of the house—the appraisal comes back at $150,000. The bank will sell the house for $150,000 and write off the $40,000 as a loss. It sends Joe a "gift letter" forgiving the $40,000 and tells him the gift has been reported to the IRS. The IRS treats the $40,000 as income and Joe gets to pay tax on the gift.

Remember, everyone is looking for "the deal." There are literally thousands of investors looking for the same thing. Be prepared to act when the opportunity arises.

Thinking Question

What actions do you need to take to be prepared?

HUD.GOV/HUDHomes
U.S. Department of Housing and Urban Development

Case Number:101-935606

Location Map

Marietta

Atlanta

Carrollton

Covington

Newnan

Griffin

Google

Map data ©2019 Google

PROPERTY INFORMATION

Address:	8898 Crestmont Dr
	Jonesboro, GA, 30238
	County
Bed/Bath:	3/2.00
Total Rooms:	6
Square Feet:	1,440
Year:	1977
Housing Type:	Single Family Home
Number of Stories:	1
HOA Fees:	$0.00
Revitalization Area.	No
Lot Size:	12,632.00 sq ft

LISTING INFORMATION

List Date:	03/28/2019
List Price:	$75,000.00 Clayton
FHA Financing:	IN (Insured) *
203K Eligible:	Yes

*Subject to an FHA appraisal
Buyer selects Closing Agent/Firm.
Property Amenities

Indoor:	Fireplace
Outdoor:	Porch
Parking:	Garage (1 space)

Foundation   Slab Type: HUD.GOV/HUDHomes

Georgia MLS   8553505
List Date: 03/29/2019 No.:
List Price: $75,000
Property Type: Single Family Detached Off Market:
Address: 8898 Crestmont
                                     Jonesboro, GA
Subdivision: Town Gate
MLS Area: 161
Status: Active
Own Condition:

PROPERTY INFORMATION

County:	Clayton
Tax ID:	05243D C007
Tax Records:	View
Legal:	LL: Dist: Sect: Blk.• Unit: Lot
Total Finished SQFT:	1,440
Above Grade Fin. SQFT:	1,440
Below Grade Fin. SQFT:	0
Below Grade Unfin.	0
Year Built:	1977
New Constr. ?	Resale
Prop. Description:	
Waterfront:	0 Ft.
Plat Book / Page:	/
Annual Taxes:	$1,088
Tax Year:	2017
Ownership:	Fee Simple
SQFT:	
SQFT Source:	Public Record
Lot Size:	1/3 - 1/2 Acre
Total Acres:	0.000 Acres
Total Acres Src:	Public Record
Feature Name:	
Elem:	Suder
Middle:	Mundys Mill
High:	Jonesboro

Public Remarks:	AMAZING HUD HOME OPPORTUNITY! This ranch style home features 3 over-sized bedrooms, 2 full baths, large family room and den. Home sits on end lot along with a level fenced backyard. Bring all reasonable offers. GCEHUD homes are Sold As IsGCY Insured (IN), Case# 101-935606 Information deemed reliable but not guaranteed. Agents please view the PIR report attached to the HudHomeStore listings prior to inquiring about property condition.
Private Remarks:	Agents must be present when property is viewed by clients. Buyers must have approval from the seller to turn on utilities after the sales contract is ratified. Submit offers through HudHomeStore.com Case# 101-935606. Use Showing time to schedule tours. Text 678.887.4955 with any questions.
Showing Instr:	9 AM to 10 PM, Lockbox Non-GAMLS Compat, See Remarks, Vacant
Directions:	Take 1-75 South to exit 239 Tara Blvd/19/41, Turn Right on Hwy 54/Fayetteville Rd, Turn Right on Towngate Blvd., Turn Right on Crestmont Dr. Turn Right on Crestmont Ct

INTERIOR

Bedrooms:	Up: O Mid: 3 Low: O Tot: 3
Full Baths:	up: o Mid:2 Low: O Tot: 2
Half Baths:	up:o Mid. Low:O Tot:O
Basement:	Slab/None
Cooling Source:	Electric
Cooling Type:	Central
Energy:	None
Equipment:	
Fireplaces:	1
FP Location:	
FP Type:	
Heating Source:	Gas
Heating Type:	Central
Interior:	Tile Bath, Carpet
Kitchen:	
Kitchen Equip:	Dishwasher, Range/Oven, Refrigerator
Laundry*.	
Laundry Type:	Den, Family Room

EXTERIOR

Stories:	I Story
Style:	Ranch
Construction: Exterior:	Press Board Siding
Boathouse:	
Water Descr:	
OTHER INFORMATION	
Owner:	
Owner Phone:	
Association Fees:	$0
Fees Include:	None
Amenities:	None
Lot Description:	Level Lot
Parking:	1 Car, Garage
Water Source:	Public Water
Home Warranty:	N
Possession:	At Closing
Possible Financing:	Cash, Conventional, FHA

WHEN BEING DISHONEST, PEOPLE CAN STILL TELL THE TRUTH. BE MINDFUL OF THE TREACHEROUS THAT DO NOT LIE.

ERIC PARSLOW

CHAPTER 12

WHOLESALERS

After years of investing, I cannot for the life of me understand why people don't check out the person selling the property. Sales are made by real estate agents, owners, and wholesalers. As with everything in life, there are the good and the bad and the just plain ugly, but I'm going to tell you why I don't buy properties from wholesalers.

First, the bad. I get approximately twenty-five emails per week advertising properties for sale. Most of them I trash, but on occasion, I will check out what they are selling. Here is one example:

Wholesale Deal: 1023 Byron Dr, Atlanta, GA

Asking Price: $190,000

Stop! Zillow this property, and you will see that the Zestimate® is $157,650. The Zillow rent estimate is $1,045.

Does this property meet the one percent rule? No! Even if I bought it for the Zestimate® of $157,650, I would need to charge rent of $1,576 per month—way above the Zillow rent estimate.

Remember the chapter on reading the fine print? Well, here is the fine print in this ad. According to the tax records, the wholesaler does not own the property.

"Cash or hard money only. The seller of this property either owns or has equitable contractual interest in the properties marketed. The buyer pays all closing costs, property is sold in as is condition, buyer is responsible for their own due diligence, and for verifying all facts and figures in regards to purchasing the property. The opinion of value is given as a courtesy only; seller makes no guarantees or warranties, express or implied, as to the value or condition of the property. The best offer will be accepted on each transaction. Please submit your highest and best offer. We would like to add value to your company by providing you with our overflow of properties available for assignment/double close. We do all the hard work so that the transaction is simplified for you to move quickly on properties that fit your criteria."

One of the most common techniques taught at real estate seminars is how to wholesale property. They make it sound simple and straightforward:

1. Put a property under contract (first contract).
2. Try to sell to someone else (resale) before the time limit on the first contract runs out.
3. Do a double close or back-to-back closing.

That is what it said in the fine print—double closing. A back-to-back closing means on the same day. It's a very shady operation and generally involves an attorney who may be a little dubious as well. This "technique" is taught all the time.

I know some excellent wholesalers; I have a good friend in Atlanta who is a superb wholesaler. His business model is to put a house under contract, flip it to an investor, and then manage the property for the investor.

Nevertheless, I do not buy properties from wholesalers, and I hope you now understand why.

Thinking Question

Why would you buy a property from a wholesaler?

CHAPTER 13

CAVEAT EMPTOR. LET THE BUYER BEWARE!

I have identified many of the challenges, mistakes, and things to look out for in this book, but what is my solution to success?

I have given many real estate presentations over the last thirteen years and always start out with the following disclaimer. I am not any of the following:

- Lawyer
- Accountant
- Lender
- Investment representative
- Appraiser
- Home inspector
- Wholesaler
- Hard money lender
- Real estate guru
- Real estate evangelist!

I am not a real estate guru, but I do know a couple of things about buying and selling bank-owned and foreclosed properties. Some folks blame me for everything; even though I told them not to buy specific properties, they bought anyway, spent too much money on the repair—and now they are stuck. I have been blamed for the mortgage bailout, the four-property rule, and last but not least, the removal of down payment assistance. I didn't realize I was so important!

I love real estate. If it were up to me, everyone would be buying. But it's not up to me—it's up to you. You, and you alone, are responsible for your real estate decisions.

Here's the good news: while you are ultimately responsible for your own REI decisions, you don't have to do it by yourself; in fact, you can't do it by yourself! You need the instruction, encouragement, enlightenment, and insight of others to become a successful investor. There are things you don't know, experiences you haven't had, mistakes you haven't made, and ideas you haven't yet gleaned, and you need others to share these things with you. There is no such thing as a "Lone Ranger" investor! (Even the Lone Ranger had a partner!)

Be careful who you surround yourself with. Who are those people in your life? Are you leaning on them for advice, support, and encouragement? Will they make sure you are aware of blind spots or hidden minefields that could hinder your investment career or compromise your integrity?

You need those people's help to grow in your investment career.

I am not all-seeing and all-knowing. I cannot predict your future, and I make no guarantees for your financial success. You, and only you, are in charge. I have a sign in my office which reads, "If it is to be, it is up to me." You are where you are today because of the choices you made in the past, and where you end up in ten years' time will be down to the choices you make from now on.

None of us is as smart as all of us! I believe in mastermind teams, goal-setting, and business coaches. Open yourself to supporting and learning from other like-minded, like-focused people. Get together with them regularly to move your life or business forward.

There is no way that you can do everything on your own. Because you can never become an expert in every facet of your business, it is essential to become an expert at building your team.

Seek out the best of the best. We do not accept mediocrity among our team and have worked long and hard to make sure that everyone shares similar ideals and views.

Napoleon Hill defined the Master Mind as "coordination of knowledge and effort, in a spirit of harmony, between two or more people, for the attainment of a definite purpose." As a real estate investor, you need to find many people to fill your team: title companies, attorneys, brokers, accountants, inspectors, appraisers, general contractors, and finally a great Realtor.

There are other people that you may not think of immediately whom you need to include as part of your team: your mentors, colleagues, and friends. Some of our most valuable team members are mentors who taught us their systems and let us ride their coattails while we learned the ropes.

Keep your long-term goals in mind and surround yourself with people who can help you get there. I believe goal-setting is the first step, and I would highly recommend you buy a book on the subject. I think business coaches and motivational speakers keep you focused on your goals.

Most of all, I think you should find an excellent Realtor who is also an investor. Ask them for guidance—that is what I did when I got started. The first agent I ever bought a house from had a sign in his office that read, "I Will Never Tell Someone To Buy A Property, But I Will Damn Sure Tell Them Not To Buy A Property." Excellent agents believe that their success depends on your success.

When you work with investors, you have two choices: you can build a business built either on a one-time sale or on a long-term relationship. If I feel one of my clients is about to make a wrong decision, I tell them—and I tell them why.

Good agents are in this business for the long haul; all successful agents build their business with referrals and by following the Golden Rule!

There are hundreds of traps in the real estate world, and I can only cover a fraction of them, but let's do a quick review of what I have tried to teach you.

Step 1: Build Your Plan

The first item to address is your dream. Turn your dream into a goal. Develop a plan.

When I decided to write this book, I was told no one would buy it. I wrote it anyway. I had a dream, turned it into a goal, developed and executed a plan.

Step 2: Build Your Team

Build a real estate team and get an education. Join an REIA.

The most important thing to think about is the people you surround yourself or associate with. There will be plenty of "negative Nellies" out there who will tell you how difficult it is to succeed. They probably tried and failed. Surround yourself with positive, like-thinking people.

Stay away from the real estate evangelists, and save your money!

Step 3: Remember the Rules

1. The one percent rule.
2. Read the fine print.
3. Never go into a venture undercapitalized. Have a six-month reserve.
4. You buy the tenant when you buy the property.
5. Beware of the professional tenant.
6. The challenges of being a landlord.
7. Property management will make or break you.
8. All real estate is local.

Step 4: Take Action

CONCLUSION

Time is your most valuable asset, so thanks for spending some of yours with me. This book was written with you in mind, and I will consider it a success when your first real estate investment—the one you dreamed about—is a done deal. It will be a done deal because you planned it out, researched it, investigated the risks, took your time, listened to your expert advisors, and in the end made your own decisions.

The first investment you make is an important one. It might not be the biggest investment of your career, but you want it to be successful because it sets the stage for your future investments. Doing it the right way from the start makes all the difference. You build credibility. You have a jump start, and you have a great launch for your next investment. So take your time, and get it right.

We started this book with a statement: 90—95 percent of all new real estate investors fail within the first year. We discussed the most common traps/mistakes to avoid as a new real estate investor.

My dream is that this information has shed some light into the corners of the real estate world, and that when you invest in your future, you will use the principles and best practices found within the covers of this book.

Invest but invest wisely, then repeat the process.

Joe

WOULD JESUS WEAR A ROLEX ON HIS TELEVISION SHOW?

MARGARET ARCHER AND CHET ATKINS

TODAY'S REAL ESTATE LESSON: SHEEP, WOLVES, AND SHEEPDOGS

Today's lesson reminds me of the Ray Stevens song, "Would Jesus Wear a Rolex on His Television Show?" *because they promise you wealth if you just pay them some money.*

Sometimes new investors remind me of sheep. New investors think everyone is honest, has total integrity, and would never harm a lamb. They are kind, gentle people who would never run over anyone except by accident. Some new investors feel they can make it on their own; one of them told me he did not have to network to succeed in this business. I shook my head, patted him on the back, and wished him luck!

If he doesn't need me to help him find properties, I assume he must be a broker and a loan officer; he must have millions of dollars, and he must carry out all the repairs to his (as yet non-existent) investment properties by himself. But I can tell he has that "five-day course, glazed eye" look about him. He is a wandering lamb that the wolf will have for lunch.

Wolf? Yes. The wolves feed on the sheep without mercy. A wolf will lie to you and ask you to lie for them; they will cheat, steal, and do whatever it takes to get you to do a bad deal. They will make the sheep think he is getting a good deal while he is being led to bankrupt slaughter. The sheep never see it coming and then BANG!—lamb chops for dinner. The wolf eats heartily and goes to find another wandering lamb.

I hate wolves (I could start cussing here, but I will refrain). The wolf in this business will eventually get killed, or at least he will starve to death. When I find a wolf, I do everything in my power to expose him. I will ensure my clients and partners never do business with him and if they do, I won't do business with them again. If they are happy to engage with the scum of this business, they are probably a wolf in sheep's clothing.

The message is simple: just do "good business."

For those of you who think this business is easy: the going is a lot more complicated than it might initially appear. REI is not a "get rich quick" business—and if you think it is, you don't need to be in the business.

In this business, I choose to be a sheepdog. I live to protect the flock, educate the flock about the dangers of the wolf, and confront the wolf. I don't merely try to run him off so that he can go and find another flock; I will absolutely kill his business. Some of the sheep do not like the sheepdog. He looks a lot like the wolf; he has fangs and the capacity for violence. The difference is that the sheepdog must not, cannot, and will not ever harm the sheep. Any sheepdog who intentionally harms even the lowest little lamb will be killed.

Still, the sheepdog disturbs the sheep. He is a constant reminder that there are wolves. Some sheep look at the sheepdog as a know-it-all and would prefer him to cash in his fangs, spray paint himself white, and go, "Baa"—at least until the wolf shows up. If the wolf knows the sheepdog is there, he will keep his distance.

Some people may be destined to be sheep, and others might be genetically primed to be wolves or sheepdogs. But I believe that most people can choose which one they want to be. Before you do a deal with someone, ask yourself, "Would I like it if someone did that to me?"

Enough preaching—here is the point to the sermon. In nature, real sheep are born as sheep. Sheepdogs are born that way, and so are wolves—they didn't have a choice. But you are not an animal. As a human being, you can be whatever you want to be. It is a conscious moral decision. If you're going to be a wolf, go ahead, but the sheepdogs are going to hunt you down and put you out of business.

This message is not to accuse anyone of anything. It's just a friendly reminder that there are wolves in the real estate business. Be on your guard, report, and sound the alarm immediately if you come across a wolf.

Remember: An excellent Realtor will never tell you to buy a house, but he will tell you what house not to buy. An excellent Realtor will tell his clients if they are getting a bad deal (on the house, the loan, the repair estimate, the insurance . . .), even if it costs him the contract.

Success in this business is easy if you do the following:

1. Don't ever say to an honest person, "Let me ask you a question, what do you think about it?" unless you really want to know what they think.
2. Always remember: just because it's not illegal—doesn't mean it's the right thing to do.
3. Obey the Golden Rule.
4. Proverbs 20:4—If you don't plow in the cold, you won't eat at the harvest.

Now—Get out there and get to plowing!!!!!

One Final Thought

My hope for you is that you will apply the principles explained in this book to start your successful real estate investment career.

Joe

ABOUT THE AUTHOR

Chester Joe Ard, Owner, GA License #218455

Joe Ard graduated from the University of Mississippi in 1974 with a degree in civil engineering. Upon graduation, he enlisted in the US Army as a Private and due to his ambition, ended an illustrious career twenty-one years later, retiring as a Lieutenant Colonel. During his time in the Army, Joe also earned a master's degree in software design.

Upon his retirement from the Army, Joe became a licensed real estate salesperson in 2000 and quickly set himself apart from his peers by being recognized as the Fayette County Board of Realtors "Rookie of the Year." Joe has put his entrepreneurial spirit and gritty work ethic to use by always finding the non-traditional niche. Joe excelled early in his real estate career by using an innovative method to assist homeowners who wanted to sell their homes without the representation of a real estate professional, but it wasn't until 2005 that he found his true calling as a HUD and REO expert. In 2007, while affiliated with Gateway Realty, Joe gained his first experience as a HUD listing agent with the successful selling of 131 HUD listings. Joe founded Vestlet Realty in 2008 and is now recognized as the foremost HUD and REO expert in Metro-Atlanta.

Joe Ard is an independent Realtor, broker, and founder of Vestlet Realty Inc.

The contents of this book are provided for informational purposes only. They are not intended to serve as the basis for any real estate investment decisions. Any tax, legal, or estate transfer of property information is general in nature. It should not be construed as legal or real estate investment advice. Always consult an attorney or licensed Realtor/broker professional regarding the applicability of this information to your unique situation.

The information presented in this book is believed to be factual and up to date, but we do not guarantee its accuracy, and it should not be regarded as a complete analysis of the subjects discussed. All expressions of opinion are those of the author as of the date of publication and are subject to change. Content should not be construed as personalized real estate investment advice nor should it be interpreted as an offer to buy or sell any property mentioned. A real estate investor Realtor/broker should be consulted before implementing any of the strategies presented.

Real estate investing involves risk, including the potential loss of principal. No real estate investment strategy can guarantee a profit or protect against loss in periods of declining markets/values.

THANK YOU !

Thank You For Reading My Book!

I really appreciate all of your feedback, and I love hearing what you have to say.

I need your input to make the next version of this book and my future books even better.

Please leave me a helpful review on Amazon letting me know what you thought of the book.

Thank you so much!
Joe Ard

www.ingramcontent.com/pod-product-compliance
Lightning Source LLC
Chambersburg PA
CBHW030716220526
45463CB00005B/2069